TRAINING HORSES

Creative Education

Valerie Bodden

Published by Creative Education
P.O. Box 227, Mankato, Minnesota 56002
Creative Education is an imprint of
The Creative Company
www.thecreativecompany.us

Design and production by Chelsey Luther
Art direction by Christine Vanderbeek
Printed in the United States of America

Photographs by Dreamstime (Jeffrey Banke, Isselee,
Sawitri Khromkrathok, Anna Sedneva), Getty Images
(Miodrag Gajic, Kit Houghton, John Kelly), iStockphoto
(Charles Mann), Shutterstock (ericlefrancais, Eric Isselee,
Goran J, Charles Knowles, Delmas Lehman, Sharon
Morris, Wallenrock), SuperStock (Juniors, Tetra Images)

Library of Congress Cataloging-in-Publication Data
Bodden, Valerie.
Training horses / Valerie Bodden.
p. cm. — (Horsing around)
Summary: A narrative guide to training horses, from
where to work with the animals, when to begin training,
which skills can be taught, and what to wear and expect
as you perform daily tasks.
Includes bibliographical references and index.
ISBN 978-1-60818-473-6
1. Horses—Training—Juvenile literature. 2. Horses—
Juvenile literature. I. Title.

SF287.B63 2013
636.1'0835—dc23   2012049916

9 8 7 6 5 4 3 2

TABLE OF CONTENTS

WALKING IN CIRCLES

YOU stand in a training ring. You hold one end of a rope in one hand. The other end is clipped to your horse. The horse walks in circles around you. You are training it!

Dirt and sand make a good surface for a training ring.

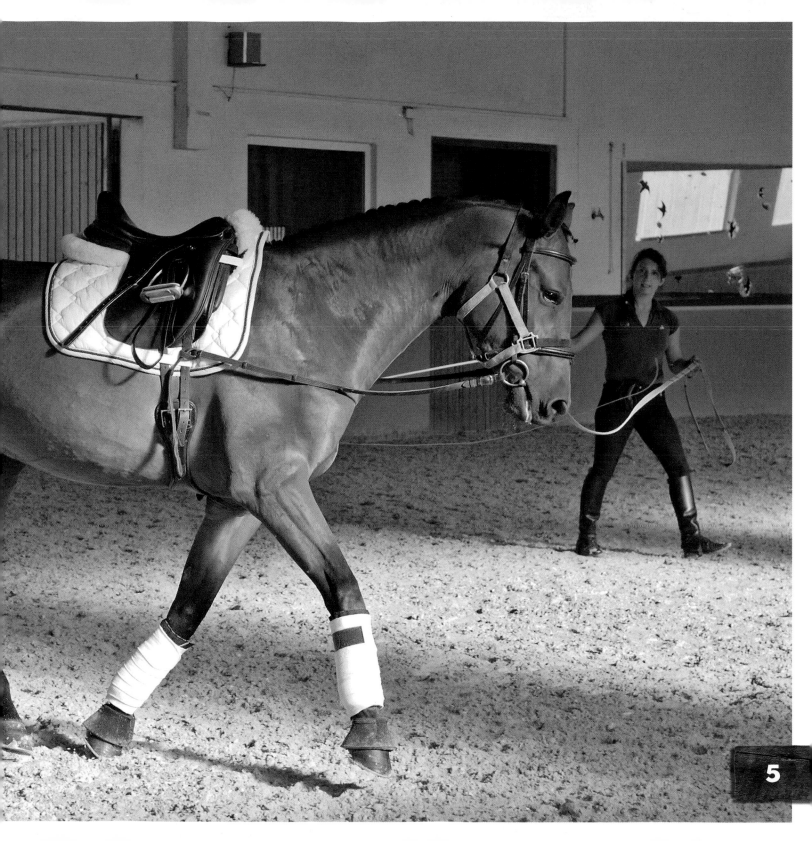

STARTING OUT

BEFORE you can train a horse, you need to go up to it with **confidence**. Touch it lightly on the neck. Talk to it calmly.

Using a quiet voice lets the horse know it is safe.

FENCED IN

YOU can train a horse in an indoor **arena**. Or you can work in a big, fenced-in area outside. Someone who has trained many horses can help you teach your horse.

A horse ranch can be a good place to teach horses.

FROM BIRTH

HORSE training starts when a **foal** is born. Trainers need to touch and talk to the horse. This helps the foal get used to being around people.

Foals are able to run a few hours after they are born.

BABY STEPS

A few days after it is born, the foal can be put in a **halter**. It can learn to walk with a **lead rope** clipped to its halter. When it is about a year old, your horse can use a **lunge line**. You hold the lunge line while your horse learns to walk, **trot**, and **canter** in a circle around you.

Older horses are trained using a lunge line.

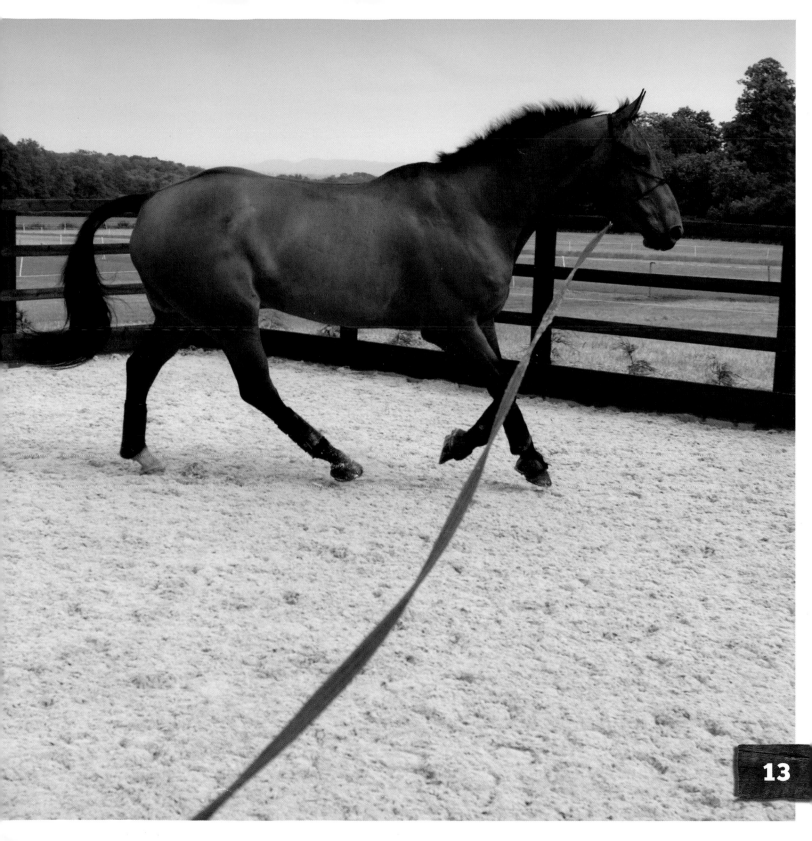

READY TO RIDE

WHEN your horse is two or three, it can learn to wear a **saddle** and a **bridle**. Then it will be ready for a rider. The horse should be led by someone on the ground while you sit on its back.

Beginners usually learn to ride on gentle horses.

SPECIAL SKILLS

A horse can learn special skills at age three or four. Some horses learn to pull a carriage. Others learn to jump or compete in **dressage** (*dreh-SAHJ*) at horse shows.

Amish people still use horses to pull their carriages.

WHAT TO WEAR

You need to wear a helmet when you are training your horse. Boots keep your feet from getting stepped on. Gloves keep your hands from getting rope burn.

People who ride horses a lot wear comfortable pants, too.

THE END OF THE DAY

WHEN you are done training for the day, let your horse cool down. Tell it what a good job it has done. Training helps you and your horse learn how to work together!

It is important to praise and be kind to your horse.

HORSE DICTIONARY

arena: a large building with lots of space for riding horses

bridle: straps that go over a horse's head and hold a bit (a part that fits inside a horse's mouth) and reins

canter: a way of moving in which a horse keeps the legs on one side of its body in front of the legs on the other side

confidence: feeling brave and sure, not scared

dressage: an event at horse shows in which riders have their horses complete moves, such as walking, stepping sideways, or moving back

foal: a baby horse less than one year old

halter: a strap that fits behind a horse's ears and around its muzzle, or nose and mouth

lead rope: a rope that is clipped to a horse's halter to lead the horse

lunge line: a long rein attached to the halter and used to teach a horse to walk, trot, and canter in a circle

saddle: a seat that is strapped onto a horse's back

trot: a way of moving in which a horse moves the front foot on one side of its body at the same time as the back foot on the other side

READ MORE

De la Bédoyère, Camilla. *Horses and Ponies*. Irvine, Calif.: QEB, 2010

Degn, Bibi. *My Horse, My Friend: Hands-on TTouch Training for Kids*. North Pomfret, Vt.: Trafalgar Square, 2011.

Pipe, Jim. *Horses*. North Mankato, Minn.: Stargazer Books, 2007.

WEBSITES

Enchanted Learning: Horse Printout
http://www.enchantedlearning.com/subjects/mammals/horse/Horsecoloring.shtml
Learn more about the parts of a horse, and print a picture of a horse to color.

How to Train a Horse on a Lunge Line
http://www.ehow.com/video_6723547_train-horse-lunge-line.html
Watch a video of a horse working with a trainer on a lunge line.

Every effort has been made to ensure that these sites are suitable for children, that they have educational value, and that they contain no inappropriate material. However, because of the nature of the Internet, it is impossible to guarantee that these sites will remain active indefinitely or that their contents will not be altered.